Also from GHF Press
Making the Choice
When Typical School Doesn't Fit Your Atypical Child

Forging Paths
Beyond Traditional Schooling

If This is a Gift, Can I Send it Back?
Surviving in the Land of the Gifted and Twice Exceptional

Learning in the 21st Century
How to Connect, Collaborate, and Create

Coming Soon from GHF Press
www.giftedhomeschoolers.org/ghf-press/

Corin Goodwin and Mika Gustavson
Gifted Homeschooling and Socialization

Jen Merrill of "Laughing at Chaos"
Challenges Facing Parents of Gifted and 2e Children

How to Work and Homeschool:

Practical Advice, Tips, and Strategies from Parents

By Pamela Price

Edited by Sarah J. Wilson

Published by GHF Press
A Division of Gifted Homeschoolers Forum
1257 Siskiyou Blvd. #174
Ashland, OR 97520

ISBN-13: 978-0615811727 (GHF Press)
ISBN-10: 0615811728

Cover design by Shawn Keehne (skeehne@mac.com).

Dedication

To my family

Contents

Foreword

This book contains quotes, synopses, and other information from real people who responded to surveys and individual questions posted online by the author, Pamela Price, and promoted by the Gifted Homeschoolers Forum through its various social media outlets, including Twitter and Facebook. All information used in this book was used with the permission of the people mentioned. When requested, we have changed names.

We at the Gifted Homeschoolers Forum and GHF Press want to assure our readers, members, followers, and commentators that we place great importance on privacy. Our community can only exist if the participants are provided a safe forum.

To learn more about the Gifted Homeschoolers Forum's mission, online support, and social media outlets, please go to www.giftedhomeschoolers.org.

We hope you enjoy *How to Work and Homeschool: Practical Advice, Tips, and Strategies from Parents.*

Sarah J. Wilson
Editor in Chief
GHF Press

Acknowledgments

This text is not my project but "our project." Therefore, I'd like to acknowledge some of the people who made significant contributions to this effort.

Without question, this book would not exist were it not for the marvelously dedicated Gifted Homeschoolers Forum team, especially Sarah Wilson and Corin Goodwin. Thank you for giving me a shot at covering a topic woefully under-addressed in other publications.

For my social media friends—especially the RedWhiteandGrew.com fans, the incredible bloggers who write about homeschooling gifted kids (particularly Dave Mayer and Jen Merrill), and the San Antonio blog community (especially Morena Hockley, Inga Munsigner Cotton, Alicia Arenas, Colleen Pence, and Debi Pfitzenmaier): You all make me want to be a better writer.

To my Homeschool 101 online workshop participants, survey respondents, and the parents whom I interviewed for this book, thank you so much for sharing your stories and ideas.

There are so many teachers—most of them public school educators—who shaped me as a researcher and as a storyteller. Most especially I am grateful for Pat Clark Bolton and Jean Bailey Campbell.

Extra special thanks go to Julie Ardery of DailyYonder.com and Scott Woodruff of the Homeschool Legal Defense Association.

Chris Barton, you always seemed to intuit when I most needed to be checked in on in the writing process.

Thanks to Casey Kelly Barton for her homeschool book recommendations at the start of my family's own homeschool journey.

Much gratitude goes to my parents, Audrey Johnston and Terry Overall, for handing me a typewriter and carbon paper when I was in grade school; to my homeschool "mentor," Pam, for teaching me that I can indeed "teach my own"; to Cathy for her enthusiasm; and to Bob for being, well, Bob.

Finally, KP and JP: I want you to know that together you are my *everything*. I routinely fall short of being the best wife and mother that I could be (read: I'm a lousy housekeeper), yet you appear to still love me despite my faults and shortcomings. Every night I thank my lucky stars for you both. I dedicate this work to the two of you together with my parents.

Introduction

This book began as a blog post on my own life as a working homeschool parent. In it, I asserted that parents who homeschool their kids are engaging in educational entrepreneurship. I also called for more stories about these parents, as well as information on how others could follow in their footsteps.

A few months later and at the invitation of my publisher, GHF Press, I began a year-long study of how American parents juggle conventional roles (breadwinners, volunteers, caregivers for young children, elderly, and disabled family members) alongside their roles as home educators. Essentially, I wanted to discover how ordinary parents were pulling off the balancing act, keeping the plates of work, homeschool, caregiving, and volunteerism spinning. The volume that you hold in your hands is the end result of that inquiry. Hopefully it will help launch a timely discussion about maintaining a career (or at least holding down a job) while homeschooling.

The discussion is pertinent because, at the time of this writing, at least two million children nationwide are homeschooled. That number rises steadily each year as more parents opt out of traditional public and private school models. While homeschooling grows in popularity, I still encounter people who say, "Oh, dear. Teach my kids at home and work, too? Oh, no, I could never do that. I wouldn't know how to begin. I'd go insane."

Using the anecdotes shared in the first half of this book, I will demonstrate that one can indeed "do that" and provide sensible advice on how you, too, can do it. In essence, this text is a synthesis of collected stories, experiences, and lessons. (Survey responses have been edited for clarity, as appropriate.)

Through my research and the experience of conducting four online how-to-homeschool workshops in 2012, I've become even more convinced that working homeschool parents—armed to the teeth with technology and unprecedented access to information about education—are part of the new breed of "educational entrepreneurs." Many of us have liberated ourselves from traditional definitions of "school" and freely borrowed and transformed ideas and best practices from various sources to craft unique, rewarding, and customized learning systems within our homes. We have stitched homeschooling into the weave of our lives, if not seamlessly, at least functionally. Our houses and apartments have become laboratories, spaces in which we tinker with ways of teaching, learning, working, and living.

A Creative "Can Do" Spirit

Long before I started working on this project, I noticed a commonality among successful, content, and well-adjusted families who homeschool. Whatever their respective education levels, income, location, or obstacles, they typically are headed up by at least one parent possessed of a discernibly entrepreneurial spirit.

Why "entrepreneurial"?

By definition, successful entrepreneurs take inventory of their assets and opportunities, organize, coordinate, tailor, lead, motivate, and, most importantly, take calculated risks with their undertakings. In fact, in the business world, the absence of risk aversion is arguably the clearest mark of an entrepreneur.

All homeschoolers take on risk when they pull their kids out of school (or never place them there in the first place) against convention, norms, and the tsk-tsks of neighbors, family, and school administrators.

They pursue home education, uncertain about which curriculum book or teaching style will work for each kid or how long they can teach at home before some unknown, unforeseen variable (the kids, the job, the marriage) changes and derails plans. They come up with the best action plan they can muster and dive in.

However, when parents homeschool while working outside the home, they risk further judgment by bosses, coworkers, and clients. They may reduce hours and salary, give up plum projects and assignments, or sacrifice long-term financial plans in order to place emphasis on fulfilling their children's educational needs in the near run.

Basically, it takes moxie to work and homeschool.

It also takes a willingness to be a social change agent simultaneously in one's home (by redrawing the lines of education and day-to-day living), one's community (in organizing and/or participating in educational, social, and cultural activities targeting homeschoolers), one's workplace (in openly pairing work responsibilities with home education), and in the wider culture.

Again, all this potentially sets one up for being regarded as "different" and inviting open, uncomfortable criticism or even outright contempt for one's lifestyle choices. Again, there is risk.

Yet over time and with the efforts of people like those profiled in this book, I predict that much of that risk will wane. It already has in many places. As the number of homeschool families rise and become more visible, we're introducing other adults to a viable educational alternative. In communities which serve as vibrant incubators of home education, homeschooling has practically become just another education choice, regarded as simply the third option beyond public or private education. The stigma is gone and the risk is diminished, thanks to the parents who went before us, many of them never dreaming that they might both homeschool and work openly and comfortably.

Therefore in their ability, in the aggregate, and to redefine the status quo, we must ultimately regard modern working homeschool parents as social entrepreneurs, people who bring change close to home and within the larger structure of society.

Who are these enterprising people?

Homeschool entrepreneurs are the seemingly ordinary moms and dads who, even though they may feel nervous about adapting home education for their households while staying tuned into the working world, approach the task with a passionate curiosity and willingness to rethink how families work, live, learn, and play together.

Sometimes this entrepreneurial spark is temporary, fading into the background once a reliable routine is established and the family is content with the process. In other families, one or both parents continue to poke and prod at the central idea of home education and tinkers to refine and improve efforts.

In the pages of this book, I will introduce you to some of these homeschool entrepreneurs, people who graciously shared their stories in the form of inspirational and pragmatic advice.

For my research into working homeschool parents, I interviewed almost 100 adults through two simple online surveys. I also interviewed another dozen parents in person, by telephone, or via email. As word about the book spread, people whom I've never met took the time to write down their thoughts and email them to me. Fans of the Gifted Homeschoolers Forum (GHF) Facebook page (Facebook.com/GiftedHomeschoolersForum) provided insights in their responses to two queries made on the page by Corin Goodwin. While most (not all) of the parents who provided insights into the topic presented on these pages identified themselves as parents of gifted and/or twice-exceptional ("2e") learners, I believe their experiences are reflective of the broader collection of working homeschool parents.

Of course, writers rely not only upon research but also upon their life experiences when crafting an article, blog post, or a book. For that reason, it's time to move to Chapter 1 and let you in on my life as a homeschool parent.

Chapter 1

Meet the Parents

Because of a life-threatening peanut allergy, we committed to homeschooling our bright little boy through the elementary years. Ultimately, this was an easy decision for us to reach: we know other people who homeschool (homeschooling is commonplace in our community); having educated our son at home through his preschool years using the Reggio Emilia method, we are confident in our abilities to seek out and provide materials that would yield an optimal educational experience; he is a bright, curious youngster with an insatiable thirst for knowledge and information. Teaching, for me, is largely a matter of helping navigate his interests.

Initially my doubts about homeschooling centered primarily on my own professional career. Having originally intended to return to work full-time when our son entered kindergarten, I struggled with the idea of how I could teach a child at home and still progress professionally. Where would I find the intellectual stimulation that I craved? How would I generate the extra income with a high-energy kid in tow?

Putting my journalism skills to work finding answers, I first sought out a few homeschooling women that I knew personally and one woman that I admired from afar.

Why women exclusively?

Because the bulk of homeschool work nationwide is performed by women.

Moreover, having grown up with the cultural message that we can and should be aspiring "career women," well-educated women of Generations X and Y and the Millenials arguably have the most intellectual effort to undertake when adjusting our personal expectations about work, home, caregiving, and education.

For previous generations, public and private schools have provided childcare options that have facilitated the rise of women in the workplace. In opting to teach our own kids at home, we working homeschool moms reassume the primary role of providing or orchestrating daycare. (For male perspectives on homeschooling and the larger issue of the daycare dilemma, please see Appendix A.)

The answer to my worries has proved to lie in synching up my work and homeschool life with my freelance work and coaching new homeschool parents. The income is modest, but the sense of intellectual fulfillment, nurtured further by the act of placing learning at the forefront of our home life, is robust.

Each working homeschool parent is different in her motivations for pursuing home education. According to the 2009 report by the National Center for Education Statistics, the primary reasons for homeschooling children—outside of religious education—include: concerns about the physical safety and emotional stress of the school environment, dissatisfaction with school instruction, distance to school, health problems, special needs, and a desire to provide children with "a nontraditional approach to education." [1]

The variety of reasons provided to government researchers suggests that the specific reasons why parents choose to homeschool are as eclectic as the parents themselves. So how do we obtain a "snapshot" of the modern homeschool parent, more specifically the working homeschool parent?

Along the lines of providing you an overview of this group of individuals, I'd like to introduce you to some of the women who have inspired me to embrace my role as "homeschool entrepreneur," by way of four in-depth profiles. Together they offer a nice introduction to real life, nitty-gritty experiences of working homeschool parents.

Emilee

Prior to our phone interview, I only knew of Emilee Gettle through an interview that ran on Etsy.com. As it happens, we share a common interest in addition to homeschooling: gardening and the preservation of heirloom seeds.

Today she is both a homeschooler and a business entrepreneur, but Gettle started her own education in a traditional public school.

"I went to school from kindergarten to fifth grade. My mom was a nurse and hairdresser who worked out of our home. We knew people who homeschooled, but I wasn't interested. I thought 'forget homeschooling.' I was happy in school."

It was in Emilee's fifth grade year that she and her family had a change of heart.

"My parents had issues with the direction that the teacher was taking the class. There was this morbid project with photographs of dead people from an earlier century. The teacher had us do astrological readings to see how they died. I started having nightmares and my parents were disturbed."

Finally, Emilee's mother pulled her from the school and, drawing upon recommendations from friends, began homeschooling her using a popular Christian curriculum and unit studies. "We did some educational assessment, too, and my parents could see that I was advanced in some subjects and behind in others."

Together, Emilee and her family discovered that hands-on learning was her optimal learning style. "My parents took me to art museums, trips, and provided all sorts of educational opportunities for me. They made everything and everyday living a learning experience for me."

Committed to educating her child at home, Emilee's mother quit nursing and built a hair salon on the family's property. Emilee stayed with the faith-based curriculum through junior high and then enrolled in a distance program for high school.

"The whole experience was positive for me. And I think it's great that now there are lots of different ways that people can homeschool [through options such as prepared curricula and distance learning]."

Today Emilee is grown and married. With her husband Jere, she participates in the family business, Baker Creek Heirloom Seeds, based in Missouri. Launched by Jere when he was a teenaged homeschool student, Baker Creek is now one of the most respected upstart seed companies in the country, having tapped into rising interest in non-genetically modified (non-GMO) foods and heavy nostalgia for old-fashioned and homegrown vegetables. The Gettles raise over 1,400 varieties of non-hybrid seeds, including many Asian and European varieties.

The cornerstone of the business is a massive seed catalog distributed nationwide annually to over 300,000 gardeners. Emilee, an accomplished freelance writer in her own right, works on the publication. "My primary role is serving as the editor in chief for our quarterly magazine, which has 40,000 subscribers." She also helps plant the gardens from which the seeds are harvested, does graphic design for the catalogue, and checks on the new restaurant. Recently she oversaw the release of a new vegan cookbook. The couple now has a contract with Hyperion, a publishing company subsidiary of ABC/Disney, which should keep them busy for several years.

In the midst of tremendous growth at the family business, Emilee began homeschooling her first child, a daughter. When Emilee and I spoke, the little girl was preschool-age.

"Throughout our busy days, she's right there beside us. She's out working with her dad on a project now. When I am editing, she is beside me with her coloring book, reading, or using an iPad app."

The Gettles are fortunate to have both sets of grandparents within a few miles of their home, but Emilee seldom relies upon them for day-to-day babysitting. In addition to showing her daughter the ins-

and-outs of working life, Emilee has her daughter join in on homemaking activities, too. "It is special to me that I can share with her how to make and take care of a home."

Reflecting on her life as a homeschool student and now as a parent, Emilee has few regrets. "I wish that I would have had more social interaction with other homeschoolers growing up, but that is not as much an issue now. I interact with other homeschoolers on Facebook. Contributing to *Old Homeschool Magazine* gives me great information, too. The biggest thing now is remembering to slow down and appreciate my daughter daily."

Looking to her daughter's educational future, Emilee hopes to provide her with a well-rounded education that is related to her own interests. "If my husband's family hadn't let him launch a business as a teenager, we wouldn't be where we are as a family."

Brenda

Brenda Burmeister was one of the first homeschool moms that I met in San Antonio, when we both participated in a large homeschool group that meets weekly in a local park.

"I guess that I always had homeschooling in the back of my mind, as an option for my kids," says Brenda, an artist and educator with three children. She adds with a chuckle, "Back in junior high school, I designed my own 'better' model of education."

That early interest in education, curriculum design, and instruction stayed with Brenda. When the time came to enroll her eldest in school, she opted for an unconventional private school.

"I put my daughter in a family co-op school, but it was chaotic. I knew that I could do a better job and save the cost of tuition. So I would say that my interest in education and the money drove me to homeschooling."

The Internet proved a valuable resource where Brenda could research homeschool options. Her part-time work and the help of her parents were instrumental, too.

"I teach art after school and a friend and I started a creative fundraising and curriculum design business. My parents are here in town. Their involvement with my kids has helped keep them engaged, I think. Of course, with my parents, I provide emotional support and help with their well-being, really more so than my siblings. I guess that you could say that I feel a certain amount of responsibility for my parents' emotional well-being."

Brenda added that her parents are willing to help with babysitting duties, and they take kids to various activities. "For instance, my father takes my daughter to her 4-H meeting. The kids also have access to an online science program at their house."

The support of her parents became even more critical when Brenda and her husband decided to separate and later divorce. "The last three to four years of my marriage, my husband was gone most of the time. I was basically a single mom. And it was super hard to do, to juggle housework and homeschool. I somehow managed to have absolutely no personal or free time."

Eventually the kids and Brenda all returned to school—she herself is now a full-time graduate student in the media arts. "The last year [we] homeschooled, I was applying for graduate school while helping my daughter apply for a charter school. And, honestly, her application was like applying for college and was a job unto itself."

The decision to make these educational changes stemmed from Brenda's marital separation. "Splitting with my husband made me reevaluate everything in our lives. When we first separated, it was in July. My parents helped me create a plan to keep [the children] at home. I didn't want them to associate school with the separation."

Prior to the separation, Brenda placed her youngest in a part-time Montessori school. "I did this so that I could work more one-on-one with the older kids." Later she scheduled work during times that her children were with their father. "For the after school classes that I teach, of course I could bring my kids with me. And that worked well, too."

Brenda voiced only one real regret about her years as a homeschool parent—struggling to figure out how to homeschool and still address her own needs. "I needed to learn how to have more self esteem or to take more time for myself."

That isn't to say that Brenda led a life of strict isolation. "I did go out with friends whom I liked, but I didn't set aside time to do the creative things that I love to do. There is an interesting dynamic at work when you spend all day with your kids, for your kids. For me, it was easier to commit to going out for drinks rather than [spending time on creative projects], but in hindsight that is maybe not as fulfilling a choice."

When it comes to two-parent households, Brenda believes that a supportive spouse is essential to the success of the homeschool undertaking, as well as to the emotional well-being of the at-home parent. "I've seen families where the husband really supports the wife in the schooling and in getting what she needs. That works better, I think. At some point, my husband stopped providing emotional support and time and interest in the homeschool cause. That was painful."

For women in similar situations, and especially for single parents who seek to homeschool their children, Brenda points to the powerful role of friends, both in real life and online. "My friends, like my parents, have been great. When we still homeschooled, they babysat or hosted playdates while I worked. Without the support of my friends and family, I don't think any of us would have homeschooled or have gotten through the divorce as well as we did."

Experienced homeschool parents offered Brenda advice as well. "One of them told me, 'focus on the work that you are doing and skip the emotion.' That is such great advice when teaching your kids: stay focused on the task at hand. I tell myself that all the time."

Other hard-earned wisdom from Brenda: "Kids are pretty resilient. We forget that. They remember, forget, and forgive things that surprise me. Once I was really anxious about disappointing my son. He had an event that I had to miss because of work. I felt so awful, but he doesn't remember it at all now."

In juggling work, homeschool, and life, Brenda notes that she has "had to learn to accept more failure and less perfection," adding that she thinks that it was "good for the kids to see me fail and move on." "Now I have learned to keep a list of the things that I do, to give myself credit for the little accomplishments."

Through her experiences, Brenda has come to believe that successful, veteran homeschool parents are accomplished at managing personal and professional changes alike. "Homeschoolers are naturals in crises. You have to be flexible and to react and respond well to changes daily. Homeschool parents think outside of the box every day."

Khadijah

Although I have known Khadijah Lacina for a few years via the Internet, it wasn't until I interviewed her for a DailyYonder.com story in 2012 that I came to realize how fascinating her homeschool journey has been.

"When I was in college, I was a single mother. I put my son in daycare, which I didn't really like," says Khadijah. "I became Muslim when I married, and my husband and I decided for a variety of reasons to homeschool."

Today Khadijah is the mother of eight children, ranging in age from two to 21. She telecommutes, too. In addition to a new job working as a sales associate for an upstart, award-winning children's book publisher, Khadijah is an author in her own right. She has three books to her credit, and two more forthcoming on Islamic issues. "I also teach in our community and online. When we lived in [rural] Yemen, I taught. Here I teach Arabic and Islamic studies . . . I do a lot of writing and teaching about the role of women in Islam."

In 2008, Khadijah was living abroad in Yemen when the Houthi Shi'ites attacked Dammaj, the village where the family resided.

Her husband had returned to the States briefly and she and the children were at home alone.

"There was no running water, no electricity, and no Internet. There were bombs going off and we were alone in this rural area. What do we do? Do we change our routine? The children needed structure of some kind, so we continued homeschooling," she says. "We did lots of journaling, drawing . . . creative, artistic projects. We kept going."

With such a large family, Khadijah has experience juggling conflicting demands and needs in a homeschool setting. "There is one major thing that all homeschoolers must understand: you must set priorities, but you also must accept that they do change daily."

As is typical of many large homeschool families, Khadijah's older children help educate and tend to the younger children. While Khadijah notes, "I try to save the mornings for homeschool," she also accepts that the demands of work can interfere with that intention. "We don't really have a set schedule; I try to go with the flow as much as I can. Somehow it all works out."

Rather than resisting reality, Khadijah has embraced the ebbs and flows of both work and homeschool. To keep on top of things for work, she maintains a to-do list. "I used to be big on lists for everything. But I'd get to the end of the day and there'd be twenty things, but I had only completed 10 of them. Then I'd feel depressed."

Khadijah has also accepted that she must nurture her own creative abilities and satisfy her need to write and create. "The first things that we homeschool moms are willing to get rid of tend to be the things that are truly for us. It might be an hour to write, an hour to exercise. And that won't work. It hurts everyone when the homeschool parents don't take care of themselves. I exercise for an hour. I try to do it alone, if I can. That's *my* time. I have to do it."

With a grown son married and studying in Yemen and a daughter now enrolled in college with a scholarship, Khadijah has positive, personal proof that homeschooling can yield an accomplished, capable adult. "Having seen how happy and well-adjusted [my son] is, I feel that we are on the right track as a family. Our kids are all at or above grade level. We don't test them, we don't push hard. They just do it. To be honest, however, when I feel insecure, I start to wonder if what we're doing is OK."

Moments of self-doubt aren't unusual for homeschoolers. At those times, Khadijah says, a mature, supportive adult is helpful to have on one's side. "I don't have a lot of outside support, but my husband is so supportive. Very much so. I'm part of an online international homeschool group, and that is helpful."

Although her sales work keeps her open to the outside world, she is confident enough in her skills and abilities that she doesn't feel compelled to compare techniques with a group. Khadijah does value finding work that, in her words, "faces the same direction as you are." In other words, "If you work and homeschool, it is best to find work that is moving in the same direction that you're going anyway. I wouldn't have chosen work [in book sales and teaching] if it didn't go with me."

Note that Khadijah's family has opted to live on a tight budget. "The grocery bill now for our family is $100 per week. We keep our costs low so that we can make the sort of lifestyle choices that we want to make," she says, adding, "Being poor in Yemen is a whole other thing than being poor here in the States . . .We lived on $200 a month in Yemen. You don't know poverty until you've seen places like that."

Jennifer

"We came to homeschooling because my son was very bored in school," says Jennifer Fink, a former nurse turned journalist whom I met via Twitter. "He was always self-motivated to learn, but school got in the way. There were social issues for him, too, on the playground. Homeschooling gave him his own way to fly."

When she started homeschooling her eldest son, Jennifer had been dabbling with writing. "I was still picking up nursing shifts, but I was also freelancing for the paper. It was part-time and it nurtured me while raising a little extra money."

Now a mother to four children, Jennifer notes that around the time that her third child arrived, she committed wholeheartedly to her new professional career. "I got much more serious about my writing. I took some courses, got more into it. The hours were still part-time, but I was selling work to bigger outlets."

Still, despite the momentum gathering in her career, Jennifer continued to homeschool her kids. "I wasn't as scheduled as some people are. I built my days around what was important to me. Homeschooling was my full-time job.

"I was at home to be with them. I pretty much took care of them as I wrote. I worked on articles at nap time, when the kids went to bed, and on weekends."

Having made the choice to homeschool for several years, Jennifer is quick to offer advice to would-be working homeschool parents. "To do this, you need to let go of a lot of expectations, you can't expect that your homeschool is going to look just like a traditional school. Work can be done in bits and pieces. You also have to accept that your house won't be neat and clean. You *live* in it."

Jennifer adds, "The practice of homeschooling is practice in trusting yourself. It is a leap of faith in the beginning. But when you do it and you begin to see it working, you gain confidence. From the moment we began homeschooling, we were constantly adapting to new situations and challenges. Homeschooling really makes you question who you are, what you value, and in the end you have the chance to create a more authentic life."

Echoing the sentiments of other homeschool parents interviewed, "I learned that to survive as a homeschool parent, you have to find ways to incorporate yourself into your day. You have to self-nurture. Grown-ups can find ways, should find ways, to grow alongside their kids."

In the wake of a divorce, Jennifer decided to return her children to a traditional school setting. That said, she has no regrets about the years that she dedicated to home education. "One thing that

I really came realize in those years is that homeschoolers tend to be living and working toward the lives that they actually want to live."

Chapter 2
Myths and Realities

In the previous chapter we saw that families choose to homeschool for a number of reasons. Although the educational choices we make for our children may differ from the norm, most of us homeschoolers are ordinary. We take care of our older parents while tending to babies, we make mid-life career changes, and we even return to school. A few of us, eager to teach our children the ways of the world, are globetrotters, too.

Let's take a moment now to unpack our collective cultural baggage about homeschool families—who they are, what they do, what they look like. This is a crucial step into understanding the anecdotes and experiences from real-life homeschoolers that we'll meet later in this chapter.

The first piece of cultural baggage that we must unpack holds the infrequent but dark and scandalous news reports of parents who misuse homeschooling to emotionally and physically abuse their children. These stories are devastating for any good-hearted parent to hear. For homeschooling parents, it's double-trouble. Such reports can fuel resistance among friends and family members to what we seek to do in our own homes. It's frustrating to encounter these sensationalistic stories, but those extreme examples serve to remind us why some states have strict, rigorous homeschool laws in place—to protect the innocent.

In the second bag is the prevailing stereotypical image of homeschool families.

Unpacking the Perfects

Based upon conversations with many homeschooling parents, again primarily women, our culture defines us as folksy, quirky, religious fanatics who live on society's fringes.

Over the last several years, many a homeschool mom has referenced this stereotype to me, bemoaning that "when we say that we homeschool, people think that's how our family lives, too." The stereotype is so pervasive that I personally have started calling these folks "Paul and Polly Perfect."

According to the Perfect model, homeschool moms are at home all day, every day. There's a lot of knitting, preserving, and gardening, too. The men in this clichéd depiction are serene and quiet, working all day to provide for their kids. They return home to make household repairs to the two-story log home that they constructed over several weekends with help from the older boys. The children are brilliant spellers.

Mainstream media plays into this stereotype. Take for instance the telegenic Duggar family of Tontitown, Arkansas, on The Learning Channel (TLC) show "19 Kids and Counting," the most famous example of a real-life homeschool family. Jim Bob and Michelle Duggar first achieved fame in mainstream media for the fact that Michelle had delivered 19 healthy kids. The Duggars, members of a conservative Christian evangelical movement called Quiverfull, opted to homeschool for religious reasons. Michelle oversees the homeschooling, but older children guide the younger children. The family reportedly built their 7,000 square foot house entirely debt-free.

Introducing the Practicals

In the late twentieth century, Christian homeschoolers took a leadership role in advancing the cause of home education. But today's homeschool community is far more diverse than "19 Kids and Counting" might lead one to believe.

In fact, if you were to meet the homeschool families that I've come to know in person and online, you will discover a rich diversity of experience and perspective. There are big families and small families. Single-parent families. Families where the grandparents are the breadwinners and the teachers. Families where a parent is disabled. There are also Muslims, atheists, agnostics, Catholics, Jews, Buddhists, and every other religious denomination that you can imagine in addition to Christian evangelicals, the group most commonly associated with the homeschool movement.

I'd wager that for every size and shape of family that you can describe, we can find a corresponding homeschool family. If it takes some work for them to be visible to mainstream media journalists and reality television producers, that's likely because these families are too busy doing what must be done daily to meet their goals.

Because these homeschool families are so diverse, there's no real archetype that reflects them. These men and women are extraordinary in their ordinariness. Most don't cook every meal from scratch. They use cell phones and iPads to coordinate multiple schedules. A few might dream of sawing logs near a cabin in the middle of nowhere, but that's probably in the metaphorical sense. (Parental sleep is a known casualty in homeschooling families.) Even if they do know how to knit and tend a garden, they may struggle to fit these activities into their busy lives.

Most of today's homeschool families aren't, in fact, anything like either the Perfects or the Duggars. Each household moves to its authentic drumbeat. They are what I call "the Practicals." They come to homeschooling for a variety of reasons and many of them define themselves primarily as "secular homeschoolers," because their primary reason for homeschooling is unrelated to religion.

A whole lot of Practical parents work while homeschooling. It may be full-time, part-time, seasonal, or volunteer, but the majority of them undertake labor outside the travails of homekeeping and homeschooling.

We have a great deal that we can learn from them, these pragmatic homeschoolers who balance work, life, and playtime with home education. You see, no matter their faith, educational philosophy, reasons for homeschooling, or income level, the Practicals face a couple of common hurdles.

Challenges

In early 2012 I began conducting periodic online homeschool workshops. Most of the participants have been Practicals who intend to work or volunteer significant hours outside the home while homeschooling. Alumnae include an online marketer, a pediatric nurse turned medical missionary, an educational testing company administrator, and a former science editor turned life coach.

The decision to embrace the homeschool lifestyle routinely brings up two central issues for my workshop participants:

- Coming to terms with beliefs about what K-12 education "should" look like versus what is the right fit for their children;

- Modifying jobs, work schedules, and even professional career trajectories in order to accommodate the homeschooling lifestyle.

The long-held beliefs about what comprises a good educational experience? That comes with experience, too, as each family makes decisions about key principles, including just how much of the traditional, eight-hour public school day they want to replicate. Veteran homeschoolers and my own experience tell me the same thing over and over: the daily schedules come together with practice—and then they *change*. Each week and month, managing the routine gets a little easier.

(For recommended books on homeschooling and sample schedules that may be adapted to fit your household, see the appendices at the end of this book.)

Adapting a work routine to mesh with homeschooling? That is tougher because it's so individualized. Yet it is doable and is a feat being accomplished by lots of parents. Interestingly, these folks work in a range of occupational fields and can be found at virtually every income level.

We know that this is true, by the way, thanks to social media.

Butchers, Bakers, Candlestick Makers

In my aforementioned blog post on home educators as entrepreneurs (please see Introduction), I wrote, "There seem to be a whole lot of writers, artists, and social media people [homeschooling their kids], but then people in these careers are prone to experimentation. We need more butchers, bakers, and candlestick makers making a go of it and chatting it all up."

Once charged as an author with the responsibility of finding people in various fields to talk about how they succeed at working and homeschooling—and finding them on a deadline with no budget, I made a PollDaddy.com survey and shared the link and follow-up questions through Facebook, Twitter, Pinterest, and my own blog.

Below is a list of job titles held by 74 homeschooling parents who responded to my social media inquiries during 2012. (I ran a private survey as a test run with a smaller pool of responses as well, to yield 99 total written responses for the book.) This list is compiled from responses to the online survey, one-on-one interviews, and public responses shared via a series of related questions asked on the Gifted Homeschooler's Forum Facebook page.

Note: the occupations listed belong to parents who assume primary responsibility for educating his or her children. It's also worth noting that of the survey respondents, nine percent worked full-time, 38 percent worked half-time or more, 20 percent worked 11 to 20 hours per week, and 33 percent worked 10 hours or fewer each week.

Medical transcriptionist

Psychotherapist

Copywriter

Illustrator

Small business owner

Etsy.com shop owner

Graphic designer

Children's librarian

Voice professor

Engineer

Economist

Academic career coach

University registrar office staffer

Chef

Childcare provider

Journalist

Pizza delivery driver

Landscape architect

Farmer and photographer

Lawyer

Dog groomer

Art teacher

Pediatrician

Photographer

Produce distributor

Nonprofit founder

Bookkeeper

Management consultant

Entrepreneur

Blogger

Writing tutor

Registered nurse

Student

Financial advisor

Social media marketing expert

Realtor

Author

Music teacher (private)

Landlord

Policy analyst

SEO consultant

Administrator for food co-op

Musician

Midwife

Rancher

Customer service specialist

Aviation professor

Garden writer

Physician

What can we learn from this list and the responses? For starters, we can bust pervasive myths about work and homeschool.

Seven Work & Homeschool Myths, Shattered

Thanks to real life parents, we know that the following myths about who can and cannot homeschool while holding a job are false.

Myth #1: You can't hold a full-time professional job and homeschool at the same time.

Looking at the list of job titles, you can see that homeschool parents do indeed hold down full-time jobs. Some go a step beyond. Take for instance Lisa, a staffer in a university registrar's office, an occupation that precludes telecommuting. Lisa wrote in response to the survey, "My friends told me that homeschooling and working full-time was impossible, especially because I was also going to school for my master's in education. They were right, but I did it anyway, and my daughter thrived."

Myth #2: Only affluent people can homeschool their kids.

Without question, ready access to money makes it easier to homeschool. Parents with full pocketbooks can more freely purchase curriculum, enrichment materials and supplies, join cultural institutions to supplement learning, and hire specialized tutors and trained, certified sitters to occupy their children. They also have greater freedom to purchase computer equipment and software for their kids.

Those things are nice to have, but they aren't required. Pragmatic homeschool parents commented online and in person that what their children need most in order to succeed academically is parental attention and guidance. Even families on a shoestring budget have the capacity to meet those basic needs. For some families on a limited budget or who must work in order to provide critical healthcare, "afterschooling" is an alternative homeschooling. It can also be used to help transition parents and children from traditional school to homeschooling as a "test run." (See Appendix A: Resources for Entrepreneurial Homeschoolers.)

Myth #3: You can't do shift work and teach your own children.

Homeschool parents do indeed perform shift work. No, it's not an ideal situation—again, sleep is often sacrificed, but it's doable. These families must first, however, solve the thorny issue of daycare.

Some do that by utilizing family members—grandparents, cousins, uncles, and aunts. Others stagger shifts so that one parent is always at home.

Amy worked evenings and Saturdays for her position as an administrator. "I missed a lot of sporting events and there were several field trips that we couldn't participate in because I had to leave for work by 3:20," she wrote on the GHF Facebook page in response to a question about working parents, adding that she "was so thankful to have work when we needed it most."

For parents who can telecommute to their job, homeschooling is a little easier. For example, one medical transcriptionist shared that she works three 10-hour days, beginning at 1:30 p.m. Another parent works full-time, but telecommutes part-time. "We have a trusted sitter . . . It can be done!" wrote Veronica on the GHF page.

What about those of us who work the "graveyard shift"? Again, once the issue of daycare is solved, parents get creative. Some utilize web-based curriculum programs, essentially outsourcing the "labor" of teaching and monitoring progress electronically. Others embrace the freedom inherent to the homeschool lifestyle, starting lessons in the early afternoon. "Unschooling," an approach to home education known for its child-led approach to learning, is embraced by many shift-working parents, too. By definition, it requires no lesson planning and can be conducted using little more than a library card.

Myth #4: You can't continue your own education and homeschool.

Parents do pursue their own degrees and professional development opportunities, often working alongside their children to complete assignments. One may argue that, even with younger children, a parent's commitment to education and personal development provides children with important role modeling at an impressionable age. It's not unusual for a parent to homeschool, attend school, and hold a job.

"I teach online. I also go to school online, and I am a freelance writer. It's hard, but I like it better this way," commented another GHF parent, Emiko. "Besides, I figure it will be good for my kiddo to see Mom working and studying."

Myth #5: You can't do seasonal work and homeschool.

Maybe your family relies on your retail work at holidays for a large chunk of its annual income. Or perhaps you work alongside several families in the agricultural sector, acquiring most of your income through seasonal labor.

In instances such as these, families can learn to adjust their homeschool schedule to accommodate the workload. The bulk of the schoolwork is done off-season. This idea isn't new. Historically, children in rural areas were given the summers off in order to labor in the fields, returning to lessons after the harvest.

Myth #6: You can't homeschool your kids until your own career is on solid footing.

There is a grain of truth in this one: the more respected and well-regarded you are in your job and profession, the greater freedom you will be able to claim for your time. There is something of a continuum, with more experienced, "in demand" professionals typically having the income and influence to set their own schedules.

As children grow, mature, and become more adept at directing at least part of their education, parents may find that there is room again for a more vibrant professional life. At the same time, the need for a higher volume of paid work can become even more desirable as college and other expenses mount. As Camille, a graphic designer, noted via the GHF page, "I would love my freelance work to increase enough so that I can continue [homeschooling]."

Myth #7: You can't homeschool without a two-parent household.

With regard to how to allocate time and money, the issues aren't much different than with single parents who send their kids to public or private schools. The daycare issue, however, can become thornier because the options are likely to be narrower.

In instances when divorced or separated parents have an amicable relationship, working separate shifts is possible to solve the daycare dilemma. When the other parent is completely out of the picture, partnering with other single parents, grandparents, adult siblings, and other grown-ups to share daycare responsibilities may work. Single parent shift workers arguably will have the trickiest time of managing homeschooling, especially while children are very young and are unable to care for themselves at least part of the time.

Truths from the Trenches

In a response to a July 2012 question posed on the GHF Facebook page, members provided stories that illustrate further the full-range of possibilities for homeschooling parents to balance work, life, and homeschool.

The comments revealed six truths about modern homeschooling families. Admittedly, the freedom that individual parents have to "live" these truths varies wildly. Much depends upon chosen occupation, support networks, and willingness to adapt and change. Yet the truths themselves remained fairly constant in interviews and in the survey.

Truth #1: Successful working homeschool parents learn how to modify their workflow to fit their homeschool schedules.

I teach online for three different universities/colleges. It is so perfect for homeschooling because I can decline contracts during busy season (science fair or summertime). It's not without challenges, but so worth it. ~Jennifer

Truth #2: Successful working homeschool parents bring the kids to work and embrace non-traditional teaching methods.

I'm a landlord. Last night I cleaned out an apartment with a baby on my hip. I also work nights while my husband works days. Because I own my own business, I sometimes have to work from home with my research and paperwork. I do that while my kids play and we tend to do paper/computer homeschooling during the baby's nap. We mostly unschool, which is great, teaching my son to follow in my footsteps as a researcher of everything. He lives the scientific method. ~Suzy

Truth #3: Successful working homeschool parents learn to let go of "shoulds."

I do childcare in my home full-time. I am a single parent, so I have to work. The things that I miss being able to do with my daughter are the field trips and things that most homeschoolers do. Other than that, I love homeschooling. We get a lot done when the kids are down for their naps. ~Teri

Truth #4: Successful working homeschool parents set and keep priorities.

I only work one day out of the home, and that is Saturday. However, I have a job with [an Internet service] and that is not full-time, but about four hours a day. I could do more if I had time. The school always comes first, and worries about the money later. It is optimal that I teach my kids to be independent learners so I can work when they have assignments. ~Melissa

Truth #5: Successful working homeschool parents embrace opportunities to generate more income. And they invite their kids to contribute, too.

I sell my goods online and work from home while my son takes breaks. He is a "more" [high-energy] child, so we don't get breaks. He's six, so hopefully next year, he'll have his own business, too. He can solidify his reading, writing, and math skills, while learning some other things along the way. ~Celina

Truth #6: Successful working homeschool parents acknowledge that "work" means more than a paid occupation.

I also volunteer and would say if you teach Sunday school, volunteer, or blog at a committed level, it is the same difficulty as working a paid job. Kudos to all the moms that "work" with their kids! ~Suzy

Having unpacked our cultural baggage about homeschool families, shattered a few myths, and touched upon some truths, we've begun to get a clearer picture of "who" balances work, life, and homeschool in real life.

But lest we paint too rosy a picture, let's take a look at the shadow side of working while homeschooling.

Chapter 3

Hard Lessons for Modern Homeschool Families

In 2009 the U.S. Department of Education's National Center of Education Statistics reported that 89 percent of homeschool families were two-parent households. This statistic suggests that it's easier for parents in a stable relationship to pursue home education. (Fret not, single parents, we will discuss your particular challenges later in this chapter.)

When homeschooling in a two-parent household, perhaps nothing is more essential to the primary educator than an emotionally supportive partner. Without it, the adults in the family risk creating a breeding ground for tension and resentment.

Take for example the story of one of the survey respondents. We'll call her "Leah" in order to protect her privacy. She is a five-year veteran homeschooler with two intellectually gifted kids.

Our journey began when I realized that my children were learning more at home than they did at school, and that school was eating up the best hours of the day. I did some research on giftedness and came to the conclusion that their advanced learning needs and quirky personalities would be better served outside of the formal school environment . . . I get most of my support from online communities, particularly the gifted ones, as they seem to have a better understanding of the circumstances I'm dealing with. For example, people without an understanding of gifted needs and difficulties would simply say to put the kids back in school if it's not meeting my needs. Gifted parents understand that it's not as easy as that. School doesn't work, so do I sacrifice my kids' needs to meet my own, or do I sacrifice mine to meet theirs?

My husband is only marginally supportive. If the kids do something great, it must be genetic; if they are a disappointment, it must be due to homeschooling. At the end of the day, my support and strength come primarily from within myself somewhere.

Leah shared ambivalent feelings about transitioning from a "modern career woman" to part-time employee and finally full-time, stay-at-home parent.

Frankly, I had to quit my part-time [legal aid work] because the deadlines were often so tight and meant ignoring my children for a week at a time while I quickly churned out a project. My husband was of the view that I didn't have time to balance [my work] with my homeschooling commitment. He was probably right. There wasn't enough money to justify hiring someone to help with the kids, and he doesn't have the flexibility in this area.

This leaves me devoting all of my time to my "project" (the education of my children), on which I spend countless hours. I research, pull things together, and generally drive myself nuts coming up with the best educational ideas for my kids. Today was day one of a new school year. The schedule was off the rails by 10:00 a.m., and by 11:00 a.m. I was threatening public school to my intransigent 10-year-old.

I get my other housework and "wifely duties" done, but the bottom line is that my role as an independent, successful, upwardly mobile, professional woman (which I once was) has been completely discarded in favor of my domestic duties. . . . I once suggested to my husband that I'd like to learn to play the cello, and he quickly informed me that I didn't have time for that.

Summing up the lessons from her own experience, Leah offers sage advice to any parent—male or female—who decides to become the driving force in home education:

Carve out something of a life for yourself right from the beginning. If you can preserve that time and space, then you can teach the rest of the family to respect it. If you do as I have, and devote yourself 100% to homeschooling, then trying to take time for yourself can be seen as taking it away from the family who may not be accepting of [your need for personal pursuits].

Seven Strategies to Preserve Equality (and Sanity) while Homeschooling

What we can glean from Leah's survey response, and similar discussions that I've had in person and online with homeschool parents, is that the individuals responsible for the day-to-day work of educating children at home crave a strong, consistent show of support from their partners.

To address that need, I've assembled seven strategies for two-parent households.

Strategy #1: Strive to make similar sacrifices of work-time to balance home and professional roles

I split-shifts with my husband—we both have flexible work schedules, plus his city job has furlough hours so he doesn't work a full 40 hour week. He goes in early. I work evenings. We do our volunteer work on opposite weeks. Our kids often go with us to our volunteer activities. ~Melissa

I work-share with my husband. Essentially, he and I together work 40-50 hours per week. ~"Beth"

Strategy #2: Share responsibilities for teaching and juggling extracurricular activities.

I co-teach with my husband! ~"Susan"

My husband and I both work full-time and continue to homeschool. I work as a telecommuter for a global high tech company. I work anywhere from 5:00 a.m. to 10:00 p.m. covering meetings and deadlines. So, I have tremendous

flexibility. I generally work with my daughter on academics early every morning. She has independent work during the day and lots of free time. My husband works locally but also has a lot of flexibility and picks her up and drops her off at activities and play dates. He tries to take a day off every month for field trips. ~Holli

Strategy #3: Share responsibility for childcare, especially when children are very young.

I have the luxury of bringing my kids into my husband's office (since we own the business) to get schoolwork done, while I run errands or take a meeting. ~"Stephanie"

Strategy #4: Embrace labor outsourcing when practical.

My children are high-school age . . . I am considering hiring an older homeschooled teenager to come tutor a couple hours a week. My oldest child is 18 and is home most of the day, so he helps out as well. ~Shannon

My biggest chunk of time comes when my children go to a drop-off program for homeschoolers that I helped found years ago. ~Lisa

Strategy #5: Design (and follow) sensible systems, schedules, and methods for keeping everyone on track.

I produce a detailed to-do list for both boys for each day so if I need my husband or the sitter to supervise school, he or she can do so easily. I use a workbox [organizational system for homeschooling] so that supplies are easy to find, and the boys know what is expected of them each day. I have a speaker phone with a mute button in case I have to take a phone call or do a phone meeting during one of my "at home" days. As my older son has grown, we've shifted to more things he can do on his own whenever possible. I schedule one week off for every four to six school weeks, so we have time to catch up on anything we might not have completed during the previous weeks. We use weekends and evenings to finish up anything we didn't get done during the schooling time. I also do all of my scheduling for the whole year during the summer when my husband is home. I adjust during Christmas, if need be. ~Kim

Strategy #6: Nurture personal interests—and encourage your partner to do the same.

As my daughter has grown and my husband's work schedule has calmed down for a brief time period, I've taken the opportunity to take painting classes and to learn yoga to provide new tools for controlling the stress in the busy deployment season coming just around the corner. I believe in giving myself outlets, as I am then better able to tend to the needs of others and keep an objective view of what I am and am not capable of as far as time and energy and investment goes outside the family. ~Amy

Strategy #7: Respect strengths, weaknesses, and schedule demands.

We utilize Sunday evenings as a time to learn new material. My children use some online programs. We have one week at a time set up ahead of schedule, but I have a rough outline of how we are going to pace ourselves at the beginning of the year. My husband works out of the home. He is able to work early and then take a break and help with anything the children don't understand, or it sometimes waits until evening. We sometimes do experiments or projects on weekends. This situation works because I have motivated children. If I dealt with a gifted/2e child, then it would be much more difficult. ~Kathy

For the longest part of a decade, my husband has had every Friday as a "flex day" on which he did theoretically keep the day unscheduled. But he is a surgeon and takes a lot of calls, so this was not "Dad is homeschooling time." I made that P.E. and independent workday from the time that my kids were in first grade . . . I also let go of my control of the day because I knew it was a stressful day for my husband. Sometimes I would get three calls with fighting in the background within the first three hours of Friday work. I am not an unschooler but figured an occasional unschooling Friday would be part of the deal . . . . So [I] worked in ski and swim days in the winter and summer, hiking and biking days in fall and spring, and I started giving the kids "self-teaching responsibilities" early. ~Mary Beth

At the end of the day, committed homeschool parents—both the work-at-home and work-out-of-the-home parents as well as those who are married, cohabiting, or divorced—should share with one another patience, sensitivity, kindness, and encouragement.

These are, of course, wonderful behaviors to model for our children. Home education is about more than just academics.

For the Single Parents

Single working adults who homeschool may be in the minority, but they merit attention in a section devoted to "hard lessons for *modern* families."

To better understand their challenges and survival strategies, we asked the following questions via the GHF Facebook page: "If you're a single homeschool parent who works outside the home (paid or volunteer), how do you meet all of your demands? Where do you go for emotional support? What advice do you have for others in the same situation?"

The responses were swift—and all from women. (None of the respondents disclosed their occupations.) Their comments echo and expand upon sentiments expressed by married homeschool parents:

Don't expect to get it all done like the married homeschool parents do. Do what you can with what you have. I go to Facebook support groups (there are several for single homeschooling parents) for support, because I tried to go to a local homeschool group only to find myself overwhelmed by all they expected of us.
~Jennafer

I volunteer from home or out of the house with the children. We donate money when we can't volunteer hours. They learn that giving to community is part of living responsibly. When I do have any time to myself, I try and recharge. I've let go of a lot because it's more important to help my children grow than "appear to be what others expect of a woman my age to be doing." I don't have a husband, my career will have to wait, there are a lot of labels that I just can't pin to my chest at the moment. I've let my expectations change to what I can do: "Mother," "Home Educator," "Volunteer," "Neighbor," "Friend." I have gratitude for what I have and what I can do, and let go of the desire to do what I can't do or be who I can't be. My Facebook home education support groups and friends keep me emotionally supported. Advice? They grow so quickly, so enjoy what "is" as much as you can and let go of "what isn't." It took a long while for me to do that and I still have the occasional cry about it, but it's getting easier. ~Tamara

I work full-time, have been divorced for seven years, and I'm as single as you can get. I recently began homeschooling my 10-year-old. It's been easy because it's just one child and I own a small business, so he can come to my office with me. I do what I can, when I can. I don't put pressure on myself; life is too short for that. I've never (until now) thought about needing emotional support; I don't have any drama in my life, so I guess that's why. My son and I take two vacations each year to ride big roller coasters; that's a fun stress reliever!

I should add that here in Mississippi, we don't have homeschooling rules: we don't have standardized testing, no portfolios to turn in, no curriculum approval by the state, etc., so that's a big reason why I'm having an easy time. The day I withdrew my son from school, I told the attendance officer that my son and I were going to "run around in a field all day long." She knew I was kidding—but maybe I wasn't? (They'd never know!) My point is that if I had to adhere to strict rules like some states have, I'd constantly ask myself, "Am I doing this right? Am I doing enough?" And I would definitely need emotional support in that case! ~Camille

We all live with my mom. She helps out, but we definitely don't do as much as I'd like. But my kids are still learning ahead of normal grades. There are local home school groups, but I don't fit in there, so I find support in online groups like [Gifted Homeschoolers Forum]. ~Elizabeth

There's not a lot of support in real life, but the sacrifice for my kids has always been worth it. ~Patsy

I'm a single mom, I work full time and homeschool all four of my children. Keeping a sense of humor is vital. A lot of things just don't get done. I work very hard to keep reality in line with priorities. As for recharging, I'm also in school full time. That does put another strain on my time, but it's my thing and keeps me going. ~Heather

I am a single mom of a difficult adopted child, with no family/friends/mental-health care anywhere in a 3,000-mile radius. I obviously don't get child support or respite, because it's only the two of us. I am a full-time teacher outside the house too, so I bring work home as well. At our house, we both share the chores, and do lots of things together (play games, go for walks, shopping, etc.). But I have also established "Mama-time," which is sacrosanct and which consist of my being able to take a bath or read a book without being disturbed— even if the house is on fire! ~Caroline

Not easy. From year to year the "plan" took some major turns. There were quite a few single moms homeschooling in my area, but we were all so busy and so tired that we rarely got together. Online support was so essential. ~Lorriann

At the end of the day, whether one is married, cohabiting, or single, homeschool parents need the support of others who share their commitment to education—be it in real life or online. They also need to allocate time in their schedule for personal growth, the pursuit of interests, and some sort of stress-relieving activity.

Chapter 4

The Path to Homeschool Entrepreneurship

Think that you'd like to become a homeschool entrepreneur? First, we must acknowledge that you will have an easier time integrating work life and homeschooling if:

You have marketable skills. If you have an in-demand skill set, you're in a better position to earn a good income while setting your own hours and personal priorities.

You sell desirable goods or services. People who own their own businesses typically have the most freedom to tailor-fit a schedule. It's also easier to take the kids to work if you're "the boss."

The field in which you work is flexible by nature. Freelancers and other occupations that allow for telecommuting have more flexibility than strict 9-to-5 office workers. Yet as we saw in the testimonies from dozens of survey respondents, even seasonal and shift workers find clever ways to arrange and rearrange work and school days to fit together. (See Appendix A: Resources for Entrepreneurial Homeschoolers.)

Your employer is flexible—or likes you personally enough that she's willing to give you a shot at making changes to your work routine. Lucky you. Keep in mind that if your employer is very rigid and inflexible with regard to family needs *in general,* you will experience a conflict between work and home life sooner or later, whether or not you homeschool. It might be wise to plan a covert escape route or a backup plan, just in case. (Talk with a qualified career advisor or coach in your community or through your alma mater for guidance, if you need ideas and strategies.)

You are flexible and resilient by nature—or are willing to learn to be. Actually, the hills and valleys of life in general—and parenting in particular—are easier to navigate when we are willing to be resilient problem-solvers, even if we grouse about it as we go along. Parental personality and self-awareness are big factors in a family's long-term homeschool success; it's never too late to foster personal resilience.

You accept that the ways that you learned information as a child, teen, and young adult may be different than how your child or children learn—and you are willing to adapt. Successful adaptations include periods of trial and error, self-awareness, patience, and persistence that may be repeated as kids progress through various ages and stages.

Of course, just because it's *easier* for some people doesn't mean that everyone else is doomed to fail at making homeschooling fit into their lives and careers. Far from it. Whenever you feel pangs of doubt about your own situation, go back and look at the early chapters of this book for inspiration. Yes, some of us are more inclined than others by nature to being "risk takers," willing to "try anything once." Yet armed with a desire and commitment to pursue a life that includes both work and homeschool, most of us can succeed as homeschool entrepreneurs.

How to Become a Homeschool Entrepreneur

Step 1: Think holistically about your life and the meaning of your "life's work."

If you don't already, begin to see your work, your family responsibilities and relationships, your child's schooling, and all the component parts of your life as pieces of one complex whole. Thinking of them as separate and distinct only reinforces the perception of conflict. Together they comprise the totality of your world and should be afforded, if not the same amount of time and energy, at least the same measure of recognition.

Step 2: Dream BIG first, then "just right."

Imagine what's possible in your life. What do you want to work toward in the coming years? What's on your "bucket list"? For specific things out of reach (living in a mansion on the beach, for example, may not be feasible if you're working part time and homeschooling), decide what appeals to you about those lofty ideas—what goals or dreams are essential to your life—and determine what can be cut down to fit. Give yourself permission to sketch out the next decade or so of your life on a large piece of paper using words, graphics, and/or colorful pencils. Think of it as your life tapestry.

Think of "eraser dust not pixie dust" when dreaming about what you want for your life and your family. Sit with your vision for a week or so and tinker with it. Ask what is going to matter most to you at the end of the next decade: a nicer car, a tighter family unit, money for retirement, travel, a better job title, a child's successful adjustment to adulthood? Consider how you can sync up the parts of that vision that don't neatly fit together.

It's worth noting that some working homeschool parents have developed small businesses selling things like homeschool supplies online. Older children pitch in and help out, learning budgets and other real world business skills along the way. Still other parents have marketed their skills as musicians, theatre teachers, and even physical education specialists to the homeschool community. Ask yourself if you have a skill that might be desirable to other parents? Could that work be something worth pursuing to generate income or increase your sense of productivity (or both)? What other ways might you link your work, homeschooling, and personal interests?

Step 3: Conduct an inventory.

A recurring theme in the surveys and interviews conducted for this book was "learn to work with what you've got." To understand what you have working for—and against—you as a parent, take some time to inventory the hard and soft assets that you have. For example, think about spaces in your community that may be ideal for you to work on your computer while the kids play. (Portions of this book were written in our local children's museum while our son played with a friend.) Consider where you may supplement your homeschool curriculum with classes, workshops, and summer camps. Don't forget to factor in your budget for homeschooling and your household.

Think, too, about your personal strengths and weaknesses as well as those of your partner (if you have one) and your children. How can you work with or around these aspects?

Step 4: Reach out for help.

Use what you've got access to in your community and online in order to meet your goals and fulfill your dreams. Wondering how to get started as a homeschool parent? Research groups and organizations and identify the ones with similar values that may provide support. Do you have a lot of bills and debt? Then you should look for a community-based credit advice service to help you crawl out from under it all. Need to make a career change to find a job that is more accommodating of your homeschool plans? Look to your alma mater or your local community college career center for free or reduced rate services.

Step 5: Design an action plan.

Savvy, successful business entrepreneurs always work with a clearly defined business plan, as do most successful homeschoolers. Invest time and energy into envisioning the next few years of your work, relationships, and home life. Consider selecting a motto or crafting a vision or mission statement or a list of goals that reflects Step 1. (Think holistically about your life and the meaning of your "life's work.") Work out step by step, month by month, and year by year plans for the next two to three years.

Naturally, when launching your homeschool experience, you will have to work with the limitations inherent to your own life, but look for creative solutions. For example, maybe it's not financially feasible for you to leave your full-time job to homeschool, but with job training or a career switch, it might be more possible in 18 months or two years. Or if you find yourself in a situation in which you really must homeschool, look at ways to cut costs and rescale your life so that homeschooling fits and the stress to generate funds is lessened. It may mean moving to a smaller house and downsizing. Or it may simply mean brown-bagging your lunch and skipping Starbucks so that your spouse can scale back to part-time work.

Step 6: Practice accepting failures and upsets as part of learning.

Perhaps it's widespread perfectionism panic, but we've become a nation of people afraid to mess up, make mistakes, fail.

Within the domain of homeschooling, this fear manifests as a fear of trying and results in a failure to begin, a fear of things beyond our control and thus a failure to learn how to adapt, a fear of our kids outstripping our knowledge base and thus a failure of us as both teachers *and* parents. But these are all fears that can be defused with practice.

Trying something new comes with a generalized discomfort factor. It doesn't matter whether you're starting to homeschool or taking up knitting: failure gets a bad rap. "Why is failure considered so bad? Besides the obvious reasoning that failing doesn't feel good; failure can offer many learning lessons to the person failing. No one wants to fail," wrote Peter Dewitt, an elementary school principal and blogger for *Education Week*. "Few people wake up in the morning and say, 'I hope I fail.' However, if failure were not an option for people, it wouldn't exist, and we all know that failure is something everyone will have to deal with in their lives." [2]

That's true, and one of the clearest markers in the business world of a successful entrepreneur is a willingness to transform one's behavior in the wake of failure, learn from the experience, and move forward armed with new wisdom. Successful entrepreneurs practice sculpting, what I like to call, their "resilience muscle."

Successful homeschoolers work that muscle—hard. I'm a big believer that during the first year or so of homeschooling, that's all we do, work our resilience muscle until it can lift us to the next level.

When working with new homeschool parents who plan to stay with the practice for several years (and not everyone decides to commit for the long haul), I remind them that the first year of formal homeschooling should be officially *dedicated* to trial and error. The second year can be a practical application of what one has learned. By the third year, you're ready to roll and fully aware that every year that you teach your kids—every year that you are a parent—is going to bring change and its unique set of obstacles.

Step 7: Cultivate a sense of wonder.

To succeed as a homeschool entrepreneur, you need not wake up every morning feeling like a modern Mary or Marty Poppins, ready to sing effortlessly through the day with your practically perfect children who do their schoolwork practically perfectly while you effortlessly pursue your own work. There will be days—hours, weeks, months, years even—where you will feel lucky if you can muster a meager sense of contentment after your second cup of coffee.

In the famous words of psychologist M. Scott Peck, "Life is difficult." [3]

Heck, yeah, it is.

And so are people. And so are some personalities. Work with what you've got.

Remember too that business entrepreneurs can be iconoclasts, hermits, and even cranks. Steve Jobs, founder of Apple, reportedly wasn't Mr. Warm-and-Fuzzy in person. He was a perfectionist. But whether they innovate with computers or with education, business and social entrepreneurs share a sense of wonder, curiosity, and the ability to scan for opportunity. They are prone to resilience, either through practice or nature, and it pays off for them. So they keep looking at the world with wide-eyed anticipation for more opportunities to test their mettle, to create new things and ways of accomplishing goals and meeting needs.

Keep that spirit in mind as you undertake your homeschool endeavor, and you will likely find the experience of educational entrepreneurship more fulfilling.

Chapter 5

Nuts and Bolts

In the previous chapter we discussed the steps to becoming a homeschool entrepreneur. Let's turn our attention to the details that you'll want to address to help fit your work and homeschool lives together.

Getting the Job Done

As we saw earlier in this book, lots of parents are making homeschool and work life fit together by using flextime, irregular schedules, homeschooling at nights and on weekends, and other ingenious solutions.

Ask yourself, "Which of those adaptations might work for our family?" (See Appendices B and C for sample schedules.)

Clients/Customers/Bosses/Employees

Have you thought about how you're going to explain to the stakeholders in your working life that you're taking on homeschooling? How receptive and supportive will they be? (You might want to share with them excerpts of this book.)

If you live in a community where homeschoolers are still deemed "weird," might you be better off "flying under the radar," not telling anyone what you're up to until you've been homeschooling for a while?

It almost goes without saying that homeschooling should never be an excuse for repeatedly being late, failing to show up for work or complete a project, or lacking focus. Similarly, unless you've indicated to your own employees that childcare for your children is part of their job description, tread carefully on treating them as free daycare providers. Such behavior will not only harm your own career and reputation, but also the public perception of homeschooling and homeschoolers in general. Bottom line: when you are in the workplace, make the work your primary focus.

Time and Space

For work-at-home professionals, it's vital to have access to spaces where you can get *uninterrupted* work done at least part of the time. When considering working alongside homeschooling, ask yourself, "How much time do I need each week to allocate to my job? How much physical space do I need in my home to accommodate my work?"

In your home, this private space may be a desk in a room with a door, or it may be the kitchen table where you burn the midnight oil or crank out emails before the kids roll out of bed. (Although whole chapters of this book were written at city libraries, coffee shops, and even in my car during our child's music class, the editing process demanded seclusion in my room on occasion with my laptop.) Co-working spaces work well if you need to get out of the house to think or use office space for private meetings.

As much as you can, it's essential to your work and your mental well-being to have some quiet time for labor. Remember to budget that time when planning out your weekly schedule. During sluggish periods, use the time to catch up on projects, hobbies, planning, and personal leisure activities.

Culturally, we've bought into multi-tasking—some of us even pride ourselves on our ability to do it—but multi-tasking really doesn't make us as productive as we think it does. Even brief interruptions can actually affect the quality of your work and dampen your memory skills.[4] So keep a practice of carving out time regularly to turn off your cell phone, shut down Facebook, and focus on business for a few precious hours each week in solitude. Hire a babysitter or mother's helper, stay up late or get up early several days a week, or trade child-care duties with a friendly stay-at-home parent.

Special Considerations: Young and High Needs Kids

When raising kids, the intensity and degree of involvement required by parents naturally ebbs and flows. That's why experienced homeschool parents advise newcomers to "commit to homeschooling for just a quarter/semester/year at a time." It's sage advice, reminding us that circumstances and children change, becoming easier, then more difficult, and easier again, as time goes on.

Arguably, the most challenging period to balance external work and personal commitments while homeschooling is when very young children are in the home. Likewise, when two or more children are born close together and still under the age of five or so, the attendant demands on parental physical energy and time are higher than with preteens and teenagers.

Are you planning to work and homeschool with a very young child in the house? Then give ample consideration to that child's needs and the impact of those needs upon everyone in the household. One parent I know, upon the arrival of her fifth child, gave her other kids a lighter load temporarily as the family adjusted to and cared for the new baby. The following year she launched a new at-home business. Everyone is thriving.

Note that high needs and special needs children (including gifted/2e kids) present unique challenges to parental energy reserves. This may make work outside the home more difficult for an at-home parent. Additional support (including paid assistance) may be in order if that adult wants to continue to advance a career.

Remember these words by productivity consultant David Allen, as quoted in a *Fast Company* article, "You can do anything—but not everything." [5] If you've got small kids—or if you have an older "high needs kid"—use that phrase like a mantra to minimize your own frustrations.

Getting Organized

Getting and staying organized while juggling work, volunteer, caretaking, and homeschool responsibilities are a critical part of the homeschool lifestyle. Every homeschool parent that I've ever talked to used at least one of the following tools to keep their families moving forward: a daily to-do list (for the parents and/or the kids), a homekeeping schedule, a weekly lesson plan, an annual calendar, or workboxes. (Appendices B and C have sample weekly homeschool schedules for various working scenarios. Additional organizational tips can also be found at HowtoWorkandHomeschool.com.)

Co-ops, Play Groups, and More

Homeschool parents frequently cite learning cooperatives ("co-ops") and play groups as providing social outlets for kids and adults. They can be great means of providing socialization opportunities, yet what works for some families may not work as well for others.

Many working parents struggle to find a good time in which to fit a co-op into busy schedules, especially if the parents are expected to allocate a great deal of planning and teaching time. Moreover, if you have gifted/2e kids and removed them from school because the school's curriculum lacked sufficient rigor, then you may struggle to find similarly-aged peers in a co-op setting. One solution is to create your own "micro-co-op" and take responsibility to lead a group focused on a specific topic for just a few weeks when your work schedule is easier.

Playgroups present similar challenges for some families, especially if a gifted or 2e child has uneven social skills. Groups that are too freewheeling and lack structure or sufficient leadership may allow negative behaviors to manifest within the group, specifically teasing, relational aggression, and outright physical bullying. Additionally, for families with food allergies who escaped public schools to evade being "that family"—the one who always has to opt out of enjoying cupcakes and birthday cakes—a large playgroup may bring up trouble.

Playdates with one or two kids present are a reasonable alternative. Focus on the quality of social interactions over quantity.

Work + Homeschool + Family = Lifestyle

As I pointed out in the introduction, homeschooling is about more than providing an education at home. When coupled with an adult parent's commitment (or need) to continue working (or volunteering or caregiving), the end product of uniting work and homeschooling is a new *lifestyle*. It's one centered on creating a sense of interconnectedness between a family's home life and the outside world.

As the persons in charge of all the moving parts, however, we parents need to be mindful of challenges on the road to building that new lifestyle model. This brings us to the topic of the next chapter, troubleshooting.

Chapter 6

Troubleshooting

Judging from comments made on the survey conducted for this book, the most challenging obstacles facing homeschool parents come in one of four broad areas: health, family, financial, or environment. Sometimes obstacles may occur in two or more areas—compounding frustration.

Let's look for a moment at some of the responses reflecting parental experiences in each area and then generate some practical strategies for addressing each category of challenges.

Health

These obstacles may include physical and/or mental illnesses related to us or our children, as well as other family members. Naturally, challenges to health and well-being may be either temporary or permanent.

As is the case with many families (including my own) who must deal with potentially dangerous food allergies, a health issue may in fact have been the primary impetus for homeschooling. That doesn't mean that issues surrounding the central health problem evaporate.

We constantly deal with [the severe food allergies] that all of my three boys have. To the point where we have to have them wear gloves when we take them in public to avoid touching things that have allergens on them. Along with this, there are little to no processed foods that they are able to eat (blessing in disguise!). So I [have] to cook and prepare meals for them all day. Nothing can be bought, for example, when we're outside of the home, so much preparation goes into leaving home for anything longer than a walk. ~Brooke

A long-term depression, a bout of flu in the winter, or a grandparent's grave illness can derail even the most structured, driven homeschool parent. Still, resilient parents rise to the occasion.

I have health issues (depression, anxiety, mild bi-polar) that affect me, but I've learned to flow with my emotions so that I can still manage my life. It's an issue of accepting life as it comes in whatever form it comes in and knowing I can work through it. I don't give myself any other option. ~Tina

[My mother] was in the hospital and then hospice for a couple weeks before she passed. I relied on the schedules I already produced so my husband and mother-in-law could keep up the basics. I let the rest go. ~Kim

In the case of long-term illnesses, issues related to the stress of diagnosis and the realities of long-term caretaking may prove especially difficult. Typically, though, with time and practice, most parents have expressed a willingness to soldier on with homeschooling. There may be concessions to health when crafting or carrying out plans, of course.

I am disabled and cannot stick to a rigid schedule. We have also missed outside opportunities like co-op day and field trips. I try not to leave home more than one day a week so that I am not too stressed to participate in our homeschool group. ~ "Marie"

Family

Because families (and the relationships that comprise and complicate them) are ever-evolving, we can count on changes to this aspect of our lives.

Often those changes are intentional (the birth or adoption of a new child) and allow for advance planning:

We recently had a baby . . . [and] since we had warning for the birth, [I redid] my yearly schedule so that assignments that were parent-intensive were completed prior to the due date. ~Kim

We adopted a toddler with a significant medical need. I have had to allow other family members (Grandma specifically) to help out with the other kids. It has required me to let go of the desire to be super mom and do it all on my own. ~"Valerie"

Death, whether it arrives suddenly or comes at the end of a long illness, can bring substantial stress:

My father committed suicide right when we first began homeschooling. I didn't have much of a choice but to put one foot in front of another each day. I took it one day at a time, sometimes one minute at a time. ~Heather

[With the death of my stepfather,] we took time off from school and did a lot of talking about death. ~Amy

Perhaps more so than any other category, challenges within the family circle are most apt to occur simultaneously or in rapid succession. One parent shared how, within just the last five years, her family had experienced repeated job loss, the diagnosis of autism in one of her children, and the loss of her own parent to cancer at an early age. Also, the relationship status of a parent can impact a family, as can the temporary relocation of one parent to another state or country because of job opportunities:

I have been a single parent since before we began homeschooling. After we began homeschooling, we moved 3,000 miles in order for me to attend graduate school. It's just my son and me (he's now 13). I talk to him about everything we are going to encounter, and about unexpected things as they come up. I think being honest, even when it is hard, is key. My son knows he can count on me as a result.
~Malea

We also deal with not having their dad around for a few months or more during the year, as he has to leave the country before we do to start training for his job (professional athlete). Being a "single mother" during this amount of time can be a lot to deal with, in addition to all of the extreme food allergy issues and schooling.
~Brooke

In my conversations with parents, resistance from family is often cited as being a psychological drain. My standard advice on this problem to set aside time to talk with the concerned party—assuming it is someone whom you regard as a true stakeholder in your family's well-being—hear them out (take notes to indicate that you're listening), and then tell them you will revisit these worries in one year privately with them. In the interim, you will expect them to acknowledge that they've been heard and to keep their fears, worries, and concerns to themselves. Failure to do so will result in their not being invited to provide input the following year.

Of course, when it's one's current or ex-partner who is resistant to homeschooling, the problem is trickier. At that point, sitting down with a trained family counselor (one receptive to home education) to discuss the matter is in order.

Financial

Obviously, money woes can have a deep impact, especially in households with budgets stretched thin. Even families who budget carefully, live within their means, and are hard-working employees may stumble on this front:

We recently had a pay cut, or rather loss of overtime, which has cut my husband's pay in half. My childcare pay was cut in half by the relocation of one of the two children I care for. All I have found to help is to cut whatever expenses we could (which aren't many) and try not to worry about it." ~Tracy

Environmental

The challenges within one's physical environment—specifically the change of address whether unplanned (from fire or natural disaster) or intentional (a job change)—can prove unsettling.

For some families, moving happens frequently due to employment opportunities or job loss:

We are a military family and we move often—every 18 to 30 months. While this is one of the main reasons that we chose to homeschool, it is difficult to meet new requirements in new states every two years. Transitioning from one location to another is tough because of reporting and regulations, but also finding a community of homeschoolers for the children and me [is tough]. ~Susan

Moving—we've done a fair amount of that in the last year and we've worked hard to keep our routine as consistent as possible with the kids. This has helped us keep our sanity. We also let things go—if we miss this or that, no stressing, we'll make up for it tomorrow or next week or next month. ~Sarah

We are missionaries in Thailand and have lived in four different houses in the past five years. We have also made three trips back to the States, spending a total of 11 months there living in other people's houses with a very sporadic schedule. I try to be flexible. We do school whenever we can. Sometimes we are finishing up school at 8:00 p.m. Sometimes we listen to audio books in the car or I read to them while they are eating lunch or dinner. Sometimes I even "make" them do school on a Saturday or holiday, especially since we live in a different country where there are different holidays. Overall, when I am stressed because we are behind where I would like to be in our school year, I have to remind myself that my kids are way ahead of the game. ~Kim

The Impact of Non-Events

Almost two decades ago at a national conference, I listened intently as a university mental health counselor described the concept of a "non-event" and the impact it could have on a college student's sense of emotional well-being and sense of self-efficacy.

By definition, non-events are anticipated happenings that come up short. Most of the time we regard them as highly publicized events. Think of reporter Geraldo Rivera in the 1980s when he opened gangster Al Capone's vault with great fanfare on a live television broadcast only to find . . . nothing.

In our own lives, we all encounter non-events. They can have a significant impact upon our emotional and physical well-being. They are often preceded by anticipation and with the perception that, if everything goes right, they can transform our lives for the better. For example, think of a pay raise or a promotion that fails to come through.

Non-events may be stand-alone occurrences or co-exist with tangible physical loss. Sometimes they may be so private and deeply personal that the world is unaware of our pain. Take for instance a miscarriage early in a pregnancy, even before friends and family have been told that a new child is on the way.

The only way to prepare ourselves for non-events and their impact on our homeschooling is to nurture resilience and an emotional support system. That may include family, friends, clergy, and/or mental health professionals if the stress of a private non-event is excessive.

Four Effective Rebound Strategies

Whether it's a divorce, long-term illness, death of a grandparent or the loss of a pre-term child, life presents obstacles. For some families it may be advisable to consider changing to a traditional school approach—provided that a suitable school program is available.

More often than not, the families that I encountered while researching this book pointed to homeschooling itself as helping them nurture their children through hardship. Rather than being a burden, homeschooling offered a means of connection and communion within families committed to the effort.

For parents facing hard times, below are some strategies that can help your family continue to grow academically.

Strategy #1: Consider switching your standard approach.

For some parents the regular routine of homeschooling may represent a port of calm. Business as usual may be a great comfort. However, some parents with a more traditional approach have successfully and temporarily embraced a more relaxed unschool approach, returning to a more hard-charging curriculum when the trouble has past. Eclectic homeschoolers with a heavy unschooling bent may decide that one or two worksheets a day help them feel that progress is occurring:

Moving to another country and back twice a year while trying to homeschool is tough . . . I try to be realistic about the need for flexibility, and documenting other learning activities (places we've been, instructional apps, videos, P.E. possibly being all the walking at the airport, for example). ~Brooke

Experiment and find what works for you.

Strategy #2: Organize aid.

If times are tough and people offer to help your family, don't give them the brush off. Accept the help. Sign up with a website such as LotsaHelpingHands.com in order to organize friends and family to help with chores, lawn maintenance, and coordinate fun and educational activities, such as field trips, to give you and the kids a break.

Strategy #3: Work with what you've got.

Life offers all of us lessons. For health-related matters troubling your family, it may be worthwhile to visit subjects related to human anatomy in an age-appropriate manner. Similarly, topics related to grief, such as cultural traditions, may be useful in the wake of a family member's death:

We've been through many stressors, including new babies, unemployment, and even having a homeless family live with us. We either go to the very basics (math, spelling) or put off homeschooling. Because we make our own schedule, we can take off a few weeks in February with a new baby and make it up in June. ~"Celia"

Strategy #4: Seek the silver lining.

Reviewing the responses from parents to this book's survey, I was awed by the tremendous wisdom and resilience that several of the respondents revealed about how they turned difficult situations into learning opportunities for their children.

They have the advantage of hindsight—it's much harder to find the silver lining when one is trudging along in the trenches—but I tend to think that the process of homeschooling one's children, of dedicating one's self to the complete and total education of them, opens the door to daily lessons that are far more important than multiplication tables and spelling.

Hardship is, for homeschoolers, another invitation to teach valuable life lessons.

The following survey responses best illustrate this phenomenon:

[Hard times] were excellent opportunities to show our children how to handle crisis. Life is not always going to be easy. Often things will happen in our lives when we need support, or need to give support to each other. We discuss how being in a stressful situation (no job) or not knowing how to help someone you love (emotional/developmental issues) can change people. Not always in a good way. I try to be a good example of how I would want them to handle difficult situations. Thinking that way guides me to make smart choices and choose my words wisely. I try not to get too emotional. Although I do have moments when I need time to think about something else . . . a trip to the movies or a fun craft together can help defuse tension. ~Cynthia

I think [hardships place] additional pressure on a person no matter who they are. I think homeschooling in general is very beneficial when these life occurrences happen. They are part of life and homeschooling is far more about real life than institutional schooling. I think these events are far easier to handle in a homeschooling family because we don't have schools to contend with at times like these, and unschooling is even more beneficial because we don't even have a curriculum to contend with. The life events are just part and parcel of school for us. ~Ann

Yes, we've encountered a lot of stressors. One day, one hour at a time, and we make it through. Will my child's life be ruined if child doesn't fully comprehend division today when parents are going a little nutso with outside stress? No. Some days, we just have to toss it all to the wind and be a family during these times. That is where the year-round learning comes into play, and so does parental balance. ~Brenda

I lost both parents about a year apart. Both had prolonged disabling illnesses before passing. Trust your friends to help. Pray a lot. Plan ahead. The more planning you've done, the easier it is to flex to more independent activities for a couple weeks. Then go back to more directed teaching later. Remember no curriculum or lesson is more important than relationships. Model and teach that. ~"Billie"

For eight months my mother-in-law was dying of cancer and we brought her to live with us during her final days. I was her primary caretaker and the whole family had to pull together to make that work. As she got sicker and sicker, the responsibilities of the home fell more onto the children. Everyone had to do their share plus mine to keep things running smoothly. We had to develop a system of my giving out school assignments in the mornings when I could and the older helping the younger keep up. It was a challenge, but one of the greatest things we have done as a family. ~Lisa

When life stressors affect our family life we turn that into a learning experience. That's the beauty of home schooling for our family. We learn in fits and spurts, not according to someone else's timeline. ~Darleen

Ultimately, learning from real life in the context of an independent-minded family is, for most homeschool entrepreneurs, both the process and the reward.

Conclusion

Now that you've heard from other homeschool entrepreneurs, read about their trials and successes, and learned ways to blend homeschooling, work, family needs, and personal needs, you're ready to start your own journey.

If you would like a little more guidance making all of this work, take a look at our appendices. First up is a list of resources for entrepreneurial homeschoolers. Remember, that's you!

The next two appendices provide detailed sample schedules for parents who are working full- or part-time. They include time for work, homeschooling, play, and life in general. Use these as a starting point, then adapt them to fit your family's unique needs.

Thank you for picking up this book. I look forward to continuing the conversation with you and learning about your experiences at HowtoWorkandHomeschool.com.

Afterword

As I mentioned in the introduction, this book is designed to start a conversation among working homeschool parents nationwide. I have only scratched the surface of the stories that deserve to be told.

Along those lines, I have created a new website, HowtoWorkandHomeschool.com, as well as an associated Facebook page, Facebook.com/HowtoWorkandHomeschool, where readers can share their stories and experiences on this important topic in the coming months and years.

I look forward to hearing from you.

Appendix A

Resources for Entrepreneurial Homeschoolers

Homeschool Resources

Making the Choice: When Typical School Doesn't Fit Your Atypical Child, by Corin Goodwin and Mika Gustavson, discusses how giftedness and twice exceptionality (gifted plus learning differences or "invisible disabilities") might affect the educational needs of your child, and considers a variety of educational choices and the path to making them.

Home Learning Year by Year: How to Design a Homeschool Curriculum, by Rebecca Rupp, is a wonderful benchmark for those who like to have broad, year-by-year academic goals. It includes reliable suggestions for curriculum materials and supplies.

What Your [Child] Needs to Know, by E.D. Hirsch, Jr., is a series of books, one for each grade from preschool through sixth, designed to provide children with basic cultural literacy alongside reading, writing, and arithmetic. In the homeschool setting, these books become highly useful, inexpensive reference books.

Creative Homeschooling: A Resource Guide for Smart Families, by Lisa Rivero, is written by an experienced educator who began homeschooling her son in second grade. Rivero is thoughtful in her presentation of "how to homeschool" in an engaging, easy-to-read way. Her advice is particularly well-suited to families with gifted learners.

Fathers and Homeschooling

Family Matters: Why Homeschooling Makes Sense, by David Guterson, will resonate with fathers and mothers who envision a more vibrant, personalized education than public education provides.

ChasingHollyfeld.WordPress.com is written by Kathy and Dave Mayer, who are proponents of "equally shared parenting." See the blog post entitled, "Spearhunting" (http://tinyurl.com/millenialspearhunting).

EquallySharedParenting.com is devoted to an approach promoted by Marc and Amy Vachon that encourages complete equality in child-rearing. (To my knowledge, the Vachons are not homeschoolers.)

Women and Homeschooling

"The Temporal Work of Motherhood: Homeschoolers' Strategies for Managing Time Shortage," in the August 2010 issue of *Gender & Society* (2 4:421-46), sociology professor Jennifer Lois of Western Washington University discussed at length the emotional and psychological challenges facing a group of homeschool mothers.

Daycare

The Four-Thirds Solution: Solving the Childcare Crisis in American Today, by Stanley Greenspan, M.D., with Jaqueline Salmon, lays out options for resolving the daycare dilemma in early childhood. Many of the strategies—including the proposal that each parent work 2/3 time— may be useful to homeschool parents, although the book is not written with that audience in mind.

Work-at-Home Options

The Work from Home Handbook: Flex Your Time, Improve Your Life, by Diana Fitzpatrick and Stephen Fishman, is an introduction to telecommuting with your current job. Also recommended are Christine Durst and Michael Haaren's *Work at Home Now* and RatRaceRebellion.com.

Unschooling

Sandra Dodd's Big Book of Unschooling is written by Sandra Dodd, who is among the most vocal proponents of unschooling and "radical unschooling."

The Teenage Liberation Handbook: How to Quit School and Get a Real Life and Education, by Grace Llewellyn, is another book popular with unschoolers, especially parents of teens.

Project-Based Learning

Project-Based Homeschooling: Mentoring Self-Directed Learners, by Lori Pickert, the founder of Project-Based-Homeschooling.com, is a phenomenal resource for all homeschoolers (sooner or later we all dabble in project-based learning).

Afterschooling

Afterschoolers.com addresses an alternative form of homeschooling that holds appeal for families who cannot commit to homeschooling full-time, but wish to supplement traditional school.

Online Support Organizations

Gifted Homeschoolers Forum
Web: GiftedHomeschoolers.org

Facebook: GiftedHomeschoolersForum
Twitter: @GiftedHF
Yahoo! Group: http://groups.yahoo.com/group/GiftedHF/

How to Work and Homeschool
Web: HowtoWorkandHomeschool.com
Facebook: HowtoWorkandHomeschool
Twitter: @redwhiteandgrew
Pinterest: PamelaOPrice

Secular Homeschool
Web: SecularHomeschool.com
Facebook: SecularHomeSchool

Appendix B

Sample Schedules: Full-Time Employment

To help you visualize what a day in the life of a working homeschooler looks like, I've assembled several sample schedules, based upon the lives of real life families, to inspire you as you craft your own routine. The schedules assume that the issue of daycare during the parental workday has been resolved. Also, the more intensive the parent's workweek is, the fewer extracurricular activity hours included on the schedules. It is impractical (not to mention exhausting) for a parent to navigate full-time work, homeschooling, and a complicated set of extracurricular activities intended to "socialize" the children.

For parents with full-time jobs, it's ideal if a large portion of a child's need for social activity can be fulfilled during the parents' working hours, such as through supervised play at parks, in the neighborhood, play dates, summer camps, and homeschool groups. Weekend activities (including church and community youth groups) work well, too, especially for older kids.

Full-Time Sample Schedule A

Designed around a traditional workday, this format can be adapted for night-shift workers. Simply reorient the homeschool activities to coincide with the start of the children's day and the end of the parent's workday.

In two-parent families, the working adults may want to alternate homeschool responsibilities daily in order to avoid burnout.

Monday through Friday

8:00 a.m. to 5:00 p.m.: Work
5:00 p.m. to 7:00 p.m.: Errands/dinner/prepare kids for bed
7:00 p.m. to 8:00 p.m.: Read aloud with children (social science or fiction)
8:00 p.m.: Bedtime for younger children
9:00 p.m.: Review math and science assignments with older children
10:00 p.m.: Bedtime for older children

Saturday

Morning: Errands and housekeeping or extracurricular activities (sports, art, music)
Afternoon: Field trips and other family-centered activities

Sunday

Afternoon: Group projects or errands and housekeeping
Evening: Prepare assignments for the week ahead

Full-Time Sample Schedule B

This schedule is built on a four-day workweek. Some parents may prefer to move homekeeping activities from Saturday to Friday.

Monday through Thursday

7:00 a.m. to 5:00 p.m.: Work
5:00 p.m. to 7:00 p.m.: Errands/dinner/prepare kids for bed
7:00 p.m. to 8:00 p.m.: Read aloud with children (social science or fiction)
8:00 p.m.: Bedtime for younger children

9:00 p.m.: Review math and science assignments with older children
10:00 p.m.: Bedtime for older children

Friday

Morning: Group projects or errands and housekeeping
Afternoon: Field trips and other family-centered activities

Saturday

Morning: Errands and housekeeping or extracurricular activities (sports, art, music)
Afternoon: Prepare assignments for the week ahead

Sunday

Afternoon: Group projects, field trips, or other educational, family-centered activities

Full-Time Sample Schedule C

This schedule offers an intensive weekend schedule and a more relaxed weekday routine. Whether you use self-directed projects or traditional workbooks as the cornerstone of your child's education, time is still allotted to learning every single day of the week.

Monday through Friday

8:00 a.m. to 5:00 p.m.: Work
5:00 p.m. to 7:00 p.m.: Errands/dinner/prepare kids for bed
7:00 p.m. to 8:00 p.m.: Self-directed project or workbook time
8:00 p.m.: Read aloud with children (social science or fiction)
9:00 p.m.: Bedtime for children

Saturday

7:00 a.m. to 10:00 a.m.: Self-directed project or workbook time
10:00 a.m. to 11:00a.m.: Snack and play break
11:00 a.m. to noon: Introduction of afternoon activity

Noon: Lunch

1:00 p.m. to 3:00 p.m.: Group projects, field trips, or other educational, family-centered activities

3:00 p.m. to 5:00 p.m.: Snack and play break/errands

Sunday

Noon to 2:00 p.m.: Self-directed project or workbook time

2:00 p.m. to 4:00 p.m.: Group projects, field trips, or other educational, family-centered activities (another option is an educational video)

4:00 p.m. to 5:00 p.m.: Snack and play break

Full-Time Sample Schedule D

Monday through Friday

8:00 a.m. to 5:00 p.m.: Work and unschooling

5:00 p.m. to 7:00 p.m.: Extracurricular activities or errands

7:00 p.m.: Family games

8:00 p.m.: Reading

9:00 p.m.: Bedtime

Saturday and Sunday

Traditional weekend family activities

Appendix C

Sample Schedules: Part-Time Employment

Part-time work schedules offer the greatest freedom when designing a schedule that allows for extracurricular activities, homeschool coops, and self-care time.

As with the full-time sample schedules, parents may want to alternate taking responsibility for evening educational activities.

Part-Time Schedule A

Monday-Wednesday-Friday

7:00 a.m. to 5:00 p.m.: Work

5:00 p.m. to 7:00 p.m.: Errands/dinner/prepare kids for bed

7:00 p.m. to 8:00 p.m.: Read aloud with children (social science or fiction)

8:00 p.m.: Bedtime for younger children

9:00 p.m.: Review math and science assignments with older children

10:00 p.m.: Bedtime for older children

Tuesday-Thursday-Saturday

7:00 a.m. to 10:00 a.m.: Self-directed project or workbook time

10:00 a.m. to 11:00 a.m.: Snack and play break

11:00 a.m. to noon: Introduction of afternoon activity (via video or assignment)

Noon: Lunch

1:00 p.m. to 3:00 p.m.: Group art or science projects, field trips, or other educational, family-centered activities

3:00 p.m. to 5:00 p.m.: Snack and play break/errands

Sunday

Afternoon: Project planning time for the week ahead

Part-Time Schedule B

Monday through Friday

9:00 a.m. to noon: Work for parents; self-directed project time for children

Noon: Lunch

1:00 p.m. to 5:00 p.m.: Group projects, field trips, extracurricular activities, or other educational, family-centered activities

5:00 p.m. to 7:00 p.m.: Errands/dinner

7:00 p.m. to 8:00 p.m.: Family time (games, reading for fun)

8:00 p.m.: Bedtime for children

8:00 p.m. to 11:00 p.m.: Work and homeschool planning time for parents

Saturday and Sunday

Traditional weekend activities

Part-Time Schedule C

Monday through Friday

9:00 a.m. to noon: Reading aloud (social sciences or fiction), group projects, field trips, or other educational, family-centered activities

Noon: Lunch

1:00 p.m. to 5:00 p.m.: Work for parents; self-directed project time for children

5:00 p.m. to 7:00 p.m.: Errands/dinner/extracurricular activities

7:00 p.m. to 8:00 p.m.: Family time

8:00 p.m.: Bedtime for children

8:00 p.m. to 11:00 p.m.: Work and homeschool planning time for parents

Saturday and Sunday

Traditional weekend activities